APR 0 8 20

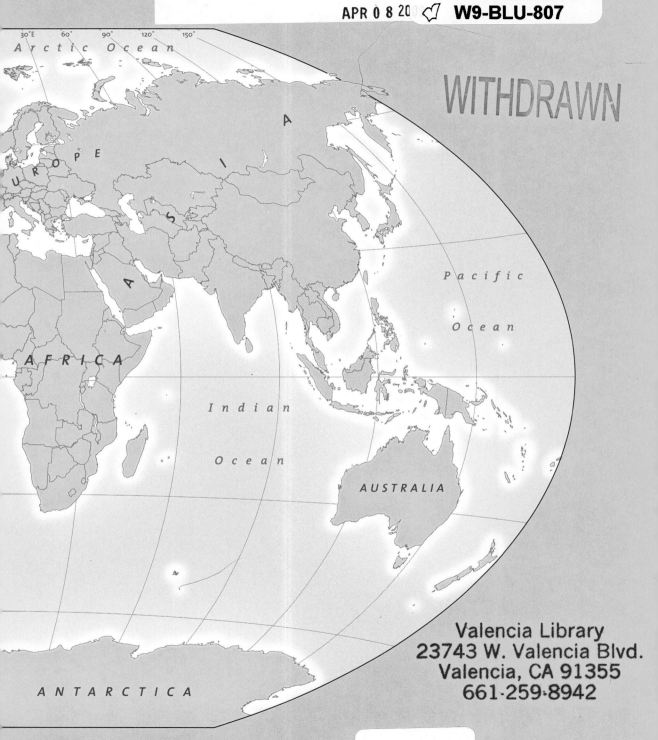

WITHDRAWN

30°E    60°    90°    120°    150°

Arctic Ocean

EUROPE

ASIA

AFRICA

Pacific

Ocean

Indian

Ocean

AUSTRALIA

ANTARCTICA

113

# *Brazil*

## Zilah Deckker

David Robinson and João Cezar de Castro Rocha, Consultants

**NATIONAL GEOGRAPHIC**

WASHINGTON, D.C.

# Contents

# Foreword

Today's Brazil is a country looking forward to losing its nickname of "the country of the future." Brazilians hope that their country can finally realize its potential. The nickname has been a burden on the country since 1941, when the Austrian writer Stefan Zweig used the phrase as the title of his book on Brazil. Since then, it has been regularly repeated. Experts often contrast the country's rich natural resources with its troubled political and economic history. They suggest that if Brazil can overcome its troubles, then it will be able to take its place as a leading global power. Some experts think that this transformation has already begun. Many economists, for example, count Brazil among the so-called BRIC countries (Brazil, Russia, India, and China) which are rapidly developing modern industrial economies.

Some Brazilians have considered the effects of living in this state of being about to achieve something but never quite doing so. Writers such as Carlos Drummond de Andrade, one of the greatest poets of the 20th century, asked themselves what it means to be Brazilian. Drummond de Andrade concluded that the idea of "Brazil" itself is somehow incomplete and so is impossible to fully understand.

Writers have been influential voices in Brazil, but the creation of Brazilian culture has never exclusively depended (and still does not depend) on literary or academic culture. Brazil has historically high levels of illiteracy, so culture has often been passed on by other means, such as by word of mouth or by images. In the 1960s, for example, movies were seen as tools for revolutionary political change. Filmmakers of the Cinema Novo, or New Cinema, movement made movies about poverty in Brazil's cities. Popular music has also played a significant role in the definition of

Brazilian identities, as have sports such as soccer. The same is true of TV networks, which are the strongest elements that bind together contemporary Brazilian society.

Brazil sometimes seems suspended between a past that is often overlooked and a future that has not yet arrived. Brazilians, however, continue to affirm the importance of the here and now through the richness of their cultural expression.

*João Cezar de Castro Rocha*

▲ **Workers complete a statue of Father Cicero, who in the 1920s brought settlement to part of the sertão. He is revered by many Brazilians as a saint.**

João Cezar de Castro Rocha
*University of Manchester*

# A Tropical Paradise

**R**IO DE JANEIRO is one of the most spectacular cities in the world. People gather on a tall peak known as the Hunchback—the site of a huge statue of Jesus Christ—to look down at the city below. Out in the bay, the impressive Sugarloaf Mountain rises up from the blue waters.

The first Europeans to arrive in Brazil were also impressed with what they saw. The official record-keeper of the Portuguese fleet wrote to his king about the new land, saying it was paradise on Earth. Although modern Brazil faces problems, the country is still full of potential. It is the world's fifth-largest nation, home to half of all South Americans, and covers half of the continent. Blessed with immense natural resources, Brazil could soon be a leading power in the world.

◀ A small railroad takes visitors to the statue of Christ the Redeemer above Rio de Janeiro and the rounded peak of Sugarloaf Mountain. The statue was built in 1931.

At a Glance

# VARIED WEATHER

The climate of Brazil varies greatly. The north is hot and wet, and the weather stays the same all year round. The south has four seasons; a few places have snow in winter. The central band of the country enjoys more pleasant weather. The Amazon forest receives a lot of rain—nearly 10 feet (3 m) a year—but the Serra do Mar on the southern coast are even wetter. These mountains receive 11.5 feet (3.5 m) of rain a year! The driest region is the northeast. The map opposite shows the physical features of Brazil. Labels on this map and similar maps throughout this book identify most of the places pictured in each chapter.

# Fast Facts

**OFFICIAL NAME:** Federal Republic of Brazil

**FORM OF GOVERNMENT:** Democratic Federal Republic

**CAPITAL:** Brasília

**POPULATION:** 183,888,841

**OFFICIAL LANGUAGE:** Portuguese

**MONETARY UNIT:** Real

**AREA:** 3,286,470 square miles (8,511,965 square km)

**BORDERING NATIONS:** French Guiana, Surinam, Venezuela, Guyana, Colombia, Peru, Bolivia, Paraguay, Argentina, Uruguay

**HIGHEST POINT:** Pico da Neblina 9,888 feet (3,014 meters)

**LOWEST POINT:** Atlantic Ocean, sea level, 0 feet (0 m)

**MAJOR MOUNTAIN RANGES:** Serra do Mar, Serra do Espinhaço

**MAJOR RIVERS:** Amazon, São Francisco, Paraná, Tocantins

# Average Temperature & Rainfall

Average High/Low Temperatures; Yearly Rainfall

**MANAUS (AMAZON RAIN FOREST):**
90° F (32° C) / 75° F (24° C); 71 in (181 cm)

**RECIFE (EAST COAST):**
82° F (28° C) / 75° F (24° C); 63 in (161 cm)

**BRASÍLIA (CENTRAL HIGHLANDS):**
81° F (27° C) / 57° F (14° C); 60 in (160 cm)

**PORTO ALEGRE (SOUTH COAST):**
77° F (25° C) / 57° F (14° C); 49 in (124 cm)

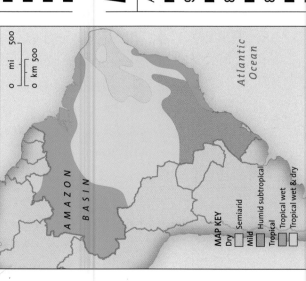

MAP KEY

**Dry**
☐ Semiarid

**Mild**
☐ Humid subtropical

**Tropical**
☐ Tropical wet
☐ Tropical wet & dry

AMAZON BASIN

Atlantic Ocean

0 mi 500
0 km 500

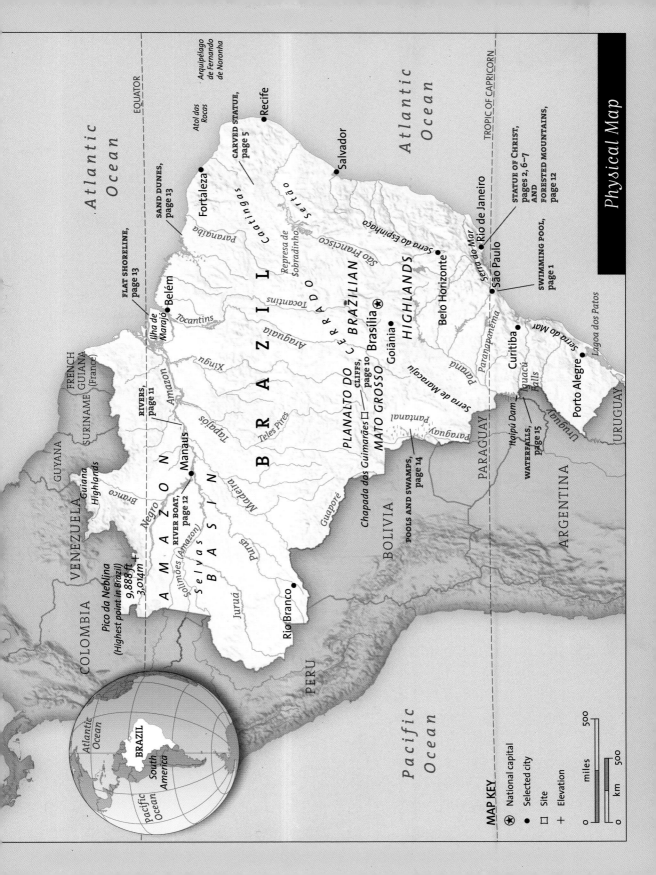

## Physical Map

**MAP KEY**
- ⊛ National capital
- ● Selected city
- ☐ Site
- + Elevation

miles 0 — 500
km 0 — 500

### Inset globe
Atlantic Ocean
Pacific Ocean
South America
**BRAZIL**

### Map labels

Atlantic Ocean

EQUATOR

Arquipélago de Fernando de Noronha

Atol das Rocas

Recife ●

**CARVED STATUE, page 5**

Salvador ●

Atlantic Ocean

TROPIC OF CAPRICORN

**STATUE OF CHRIST, pages 2, 6–7, AND FORESTED MOUNTAINS, page 12**

Rio de Janeiro ●

Serra do Mar

São Paulo ●

**SWIMMING POOL, page 1**

Belo Horizonte ●

Serra do Espinhaço

São Francisco

Represa de Sobradinho

sertão

Caatingas

Paranaíba

Fortaleza ●

**SAND DUNES, page 13**

**FLAT SHORELINE, page 13**

Ilha de Marajó

Belém ●

Tocantins

Tocantins

Araguaia

CERRADO

BRAZILIAN HIGHLANDS

Brasília ⊛

Goiânia ●

Paraná

Paranapanema

Serra do Mar

Curitiba ●

Iguaçú Falls

**WATERFALLS, page 15**

Itaipú Dam

Uruguai

Porto Alegre ●

Lagoa dos Patos

PARAGUAY

ARGENTINA

URUGUAY

Serra de Maracaju

Paraguay

Pantanal

**POOLS AND SWAMPS, page 14**

Chapada dos Guimarães ☐

**CLIFFS, page 10**

PLANALTO DO MATO GROSSO

B R A Z I L

Teles Pires

Tapajós

Xingu

Amazon

**RIVERS, page 11**

Negro

Branco

Guiana Highlands

VENEZUELA

COLOMBIA

Pico da Neblina (Highest point in Brazil) 9,888 ft 3,014 m +

Solimões (Amazon)

S e l v a s

A M A Z O N B A S I N

Manaus ●

**RIVER BOAT, page 12**

Juruá

Purus

Madeira

Guaporé

Rio Branco ●

BOLIVIA

PERU

Pacific Ocean

GUYANA

SURINAME

FRENCH GUIANA (France)

▲ The cliffs of the Chapada dos Guimarães in western Brazil mark the meeting between the lowland rain forests of the Amazon and the grassy uplands of central Brazil.

# A Big Country

Brazil is the largest country in South America. It forms a triangle shape that stretches 2,684 miles (4,319 km) from east to west and 2,731 miles (4,394 km) from north to south. To the east Brazil has a 4,500-mile (7,367 km) coastline along the Atlantic Ocean. In the other directions, it has borders with every other South American country except Chile and Ecuador.

Covering so much area, the Brazilian landscape is very varied. The northwest is filled with the world's largest jungle, but elsewhere there are dry grasslands, rugged hills, immense plateaus, and a long coastal plain. Brazil can be divided into five zones: the north, northeast, center-west, southeast, and south.

# The River Sea

The north of Brazil is dominated by the Amazon River. The river's basin covers 45 percent of Brazil and extends north and west into most of the neighboring countries. The Amazon is not one river but a network of many hundreds, and it is difficult to pinpoint where it begins. In 2007, a small river starting high in the mountains of Peru was found to run into the Amazon. That gives the Amazon a total length of 4,250 miles (6,840 km), making it the longest river on Earth. The Amazon is also by far the largest river. It carries one-fifth of all the world's river water. There is so much water in the basin that the Brazilians sometimes refer to the Amazon as the River Sea. By the time it reaches the ocean at Belém on Brazil's east coast, the river is 207 miles (330 km) wide.

## *Inland Waterway*

There are no bridges over the Amazon; it is too wide near its mouth, and in the jungles upstream there are no roads that need bridges. Ocean-going ships can sail from the Atlantic into the heart of the forest. The river's main channel is formed at Manaus, a major city, where two large rivers meet. Although it is 1,000 miles (1,600 km) from the sea, Manaus has a busy port. Smaller boats can travel upstream from there as far as Iquitos over the border in Peru, which is 2,240 miles (3,600 km) from the Atlantic: It is only 470 miles (756 km) overland in the other direction to the Pacific Ocean!

▲ Two rivers meet within the Amazon rain forest on their way to the main river. Local people say that the land and water are reversed in the Amazon—the rivers are the roads, while the jungle is an ocean of trees too thick to cross.

▲ The Tijuca Forest grows on hills at the heart of Rio de Janeiro. The forest contains many threatened species from the Atlantic forest.

Manaus is only 144 feet (44 m) above sea level, even though it is so far inland. The Amazon Basin is almost completely flat. As a result, the high tide from the ocean surges far up the river. The tide forms a wave up to 30 feet (9 m) high. The wave—called *pororoca*, or "big roar," for the noise it makes—travels 180 miles (300 km) inland.

## Old Brazil

The northeast region forms the Brazilian bulge, which sticks out into the Atlantic. The coast of the bulge is the *zona da mata*, or Atlantic forest. The inland is too dry for forest and becomes the sertão, a dry grassland. Although rainfall is low in the sertão, the region has been transformed into green fields by a network of irrigation channels. Much of the water comes from the São Francisco River, the second longest in Brazil, which flows to the south.

## THE MEETING OF THE WATERS

The muddy waters of the Solimões River meet the clear water of the Negro River close to the city of Manaus to form the Amazon. When the waters meet, however, they do not immediately mix. For miles the waters flow alongside each other (below). Manaus is one of the most isolated cities on the planet—just two roads connect it to the outside world. It serves as the gateway to the Amazon region, but traffic arrives only by river or air.

## ISLAND IN THE RIVER

▲ Marajó is a little larger than the U.S. state of Maryland.

At the mouth of the Amazon is the Ilha de Marajó, the world's largest river island. The island has little traffic. The roads that exist are built on stilts 10 feet (3 m) above the ground because floods regularly sweep over the flat landscape. For many islanders the easiest way to get around is by buffalo. Water buffaloes were introduced to the island about 70 years ago.

Marajó was first settled by Europeans when Portuguese monks arrived there in 1617. There is archaeological evidence that before the Europeans arrived, Native Americans also once lived on the island.

The northeast was the first area to be colonized by Europeans in the 16th century. The settlers built the historic cities of Salvador and Recife on the coast. About a third of Brazil's population still lives in the area.

## A Wilderness

The center-west lies south of the Amazon and is dominated by the highlands that rise from the river to form a plateau about 3,280 feet (1,000 m) high. Like the jungle to the north, the center-west is another vast

▼ Tourists are dwarfed by the towering dunes of Lençóis Maranhenses National Park on the northeastern coast.

wilderness, but this time of grass and bushes. It is known as the *cerrado*. It also includes the Pantanal wetlands in the west. The cerrado is mainly covered by huge cattle ranches and there are also rich reserves of metals and minerals underground. In the 1960s, a new capital city, Brasília, was built in the cerrado as a way of encouraging more people to move there.

## A Country in Itself

The southeast covers only 11 percent of Brazil but is home to 43 percent of Brazilians, making it by far the most crowded area of the country. Originally, it was covered with thick Atlantic forest, but today 80 percent of the trees have been cleared. The southeast is the

## WET FEET

Covering an area about the size of Kentucky, the Pantanal in central Brazil is the world's largest wetland. Every summer, the waters of the River Paraguay rise by 16 feet (5 meters) and flood the area. The Pantanal is home to an amazing wealth of wildlife; it also has the world's richest variety of water flowers.

The Pantanal's economy is based on ranching and agriculture. Soy, rice, and corn are the main crops, but eco-tourism has also become a big business. Wildlife is easier to spot there than in the dense Amazon rain forest. Part of the Pantanal area is now a national park, where hunting and fishing are controlled.

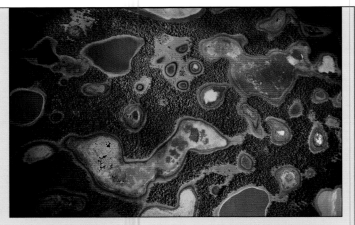

▲ The Pantanal is a patchwork of flooded lagoons and small islands.

## THE DEVIL'S THROAT

Brazil has many mighty rivers—and hundreds of waterfalls. The remarkable Iguaçu Falls are the largest falls in the world. They are shared between Brazil and Argentina and are actually made up of 275 waterfalls, all of which are over 270 feet (80 meters) tall. The falls plunge off a cliff that is 2 miles (3 km) wide. At the spectacular *Garganta do Diabo*—Devil's Throat—the water from 14 waterfalls joins to pound the rocks below with a continuous roar.

▲ Tourists look at the falls from the Brazilian side of the Devil's Throat.

industrial center of Brazil. Brazil's biggest city, São Paulo, is home to half the country's industry. Rio de Janeiro—the former capital—is the most famous of Brazilian cities. It is a thriving cultural center set between ocean and mountains. Despite the success of Brazil's cities, however, they are surrounded by *favelas*, large slum districts where standards of living are poor.

## Little Europe

The south is the smallest region. It is often compared to Europe. Not only is the region's climate cooler than that of the rest of Brazil, but it is also home to many Germans and Italians, who have left their mark. The coastal cities are industrial centers. Away from the coast, the region is filled with pine forests and vast prairies, or *pampas*, which extend into Paraguay and Argentina.

▼ São Paulo is the largest city in Brazil— and one of the largest in the world. More than 11 million people live there.

# Wonderful Wildlife

**B**RAZIL HAS THE GREATEST VARIETY of animals of any country in the world. There are about 600 species of mammals, many of which are unlike anything living elsewhere. The forests are home to sluggish sloths and 30 types of monkeys, including the pygmy marmoset, the world's tiniest monkey. In the rivers live pink-skinned dolphins and giant rodents called capybaras—along with at least 1,500 species of fish. Brazil has more types of birds than any other country—1,600 species. There are many reptile species, too, including five types of alligators. With 3,000 different species living in every square mile (2.6 sq km) of forest, biologists are discovering new species all the time: 100,000 different insects and other bugs have been listed so far!

◄ A colorful songbird hitches a ride on the head of a capybara wading through a swamp thick with water plants. Capybaras are giant relatives of guinea pigs.

# WILDLIFE ZONES

**B**razil is thought to be home to 70 percent of the world's animal species. Most live in the world's largest jungle, the Amazon rain forest. But not all of Brazil is made up of jungle. About 60 percent of the country is covered in grasslands (or pampas), pine forests, and semideserts. In addition to the Amazon Basin, lush rain forests grow along parts of the Atlantic coastline where rainfall is also very heavy. The map opposite shows the main vegetation zones—what grows where in Brazil. Each zone is home to a distinct group of plants and animals.

▲ At 6 feet (1.8 m) long, Brazil's giant otters are the largest in the world. They hunt in the water for fish and crabs, but also attack baby caimans (alligators).

# Species at Risk

**M**odern Brazil has the difficult task of protecting the habitats of its world-famous wildlife while continuing to develop its economy and build new towns for its growing population. Today 7.3 percent of the country's area is protected through a network of national parks, reserves, and refuges. Building of any kind is banned on 3.3 percent of this land, while the remaining 4 percent is being developed in a way that does not damage the environment. The Brazilian environmental agency, Instituto Brasileiro do Meio Ambiente (IBAMA), lists 395 endangered species. These include 160 birds, 96 insects, 69 mammals, 34 invertebrates, 20 reptiles, and 16 amphibians. A separate survey lists 166 fish as endangered.

Species at risk include:

> Bare-faced curassow (bird)
> Boto (dolphin)
> Bush dog
> Giant armadillo
> Giant otter
> Golden parakeet
> Greater flamingo
> Harpy eagle
> Hyacinth macaw (bird)
> Jaguar
> Manatee (sea cow)
> Maned wolf
> Margay (cat)
> Muriquis (monkey)
> Pied tamarin (monkey)
> Spider monkey

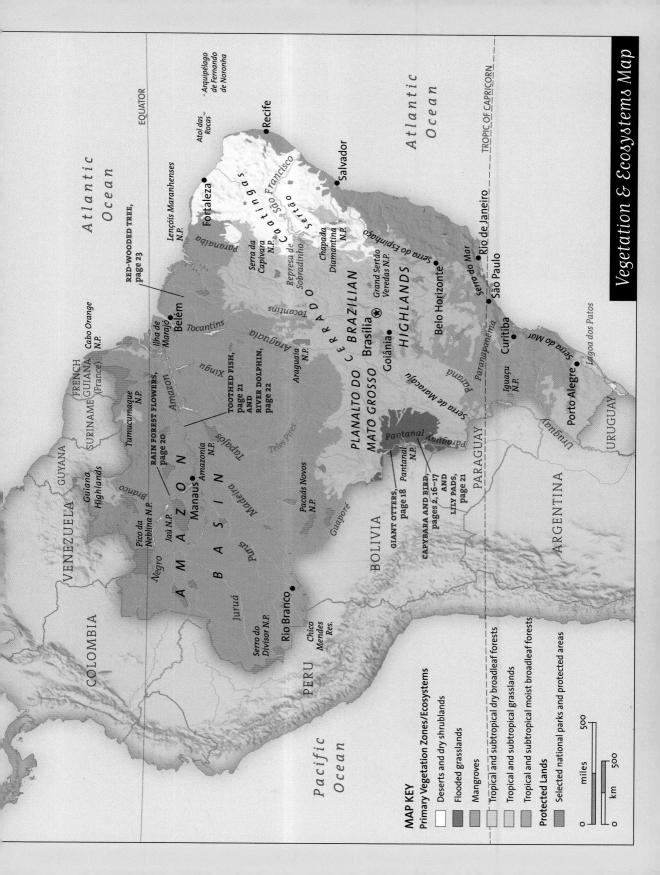

# Vegetation & Ecosystems Map

**Atlantic Ocean**

EQUATOR

Arquipélago de Fernando de Noronha

Atol das Rocas

Recife

Fortaleza

Lençóis Maranhenses N.P.

**RED-WOODED TREE, page 23**

Serra da Capivara N.P.

Represa de Sobradinho

Chapada Diamantina N.P.

Caatinga

Sertão

São Francisco

Parnaíba

Salvador

Atlantic Ocean

TROPIC OF CAPRICORN

Grand Sertão Veredas N.P.

Serra do Espinhaço

Serra do Mar

Rio de Janeiro

São Paulo

HIGHLANDS

Belo Horizonte

BRAZILIAN

Brasília

Goiânia

PLANALTO DO CERRADO

MATO GROSSO

Tocantins

Araguaia

Araguaia N.P.

Paraná

Paranapanema

Curitiba

Iguaçu N.P.

Serra do Mar

Porto Alegre

Lagoa dos Patos

Serra de Maracaju

Paraguay

Pantanal

Pantanal N.P.

**GIANT OTTERS, page 18**

**CAPYBARA AND BIRD, pages 2, 16–17 AND LILY PADS, page 21**

BOLIVIA

PARAGUAY

ARGENTINA

URUGUAY

Uruguay

Belém

Ilha de Marajó

Tocantins

Cabo Orange N.P.

FRENCH GUIANA (France)

SURINAME

GUYANA

Tumucumaque N.P.

Xingu

Amazon

Tapajós

Teles Pires

**RAIN FOREST FLOWERS, page 20**

**TOOTHED FISH, page 21 AND RIVER DOLPHIN, page 22**

Amazônia N.P.

Pacaás Novos N.P.

Guaporé

Madeira

Purus

Manaus

AMAZON BASIN

Jaú N.P.

Pico da Neblina N.P.

Branco

Negro

Guiana Highlands

VENEZUELA

COLOMBIA

PERU

Juruá

Serra do Divisor N.P.

Rio Branco

Chico Mendes Res.

Pacific Ocean

**MAP KEY**

**Primary Vegetation Zones/Ecosystems**

- Deserts and dry shrublands
- Flooded grasslands
- Mangroves
- Tropical and subtropical dry broadleaf forests
- Tropical and subtropical grasslands
- Tropical and subtropical moist broadleaf forests

**Protected Lands**

- Selected national parks and protected areas

miles 0 500

km 0 500

▲ Flowers bloom at the tops of rain-forest trees. It is too crowded and dark for flowers to grow beneath the canopy.

▼ The hyacinth macaw is the largest flying parrot in the world.

# Human Impact

From prehistoric times, people have been changing the environment of Brazil. Amerindians, for example, cleared patches in the forest for growing crops. But when settlers from Europe arrived in the 1500s the destruction got a lot worse. The colonizers started to cut down the coastal forests to export wood to Europe. The Atlantic rain forest has never really recovered. Less than 8 percent of it remains. In the past 200 years, the destruction has spread inland. Every ten years an area of rain forest twice the size of Portugal is cut down in the Amazon. The trees are used for wood and the land is then cleared to make way for farmland. Rain-forest species are unable to survive outside of the jungle and many are now close to extinction.

# Largest Forest

The Amazon remains the largest forest on the planet—half of which is in Brazil. In the 1960s and 1970s government programs aimed to turn the Amazon into farms without any concern for the environment. In recent years, however, conservation measures have slowed the rate of deforestation.

# KILLER FISH OF THE AMAZON

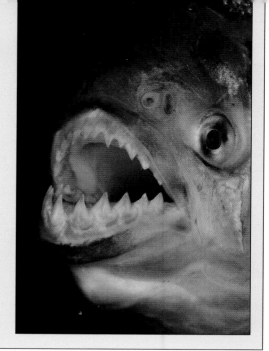

**P**iranhas live only in the Amazon and a few other South American rivers. They are notorious for their sharp teeth; a school of piranhas can strip prey to its bones within a few minutes, turning the river red with blood. However, the piranha is often not as ferocious as its image suggests. They become aggressive only when a crowd forms around the body of a large dead animal. Of the 30 species of piranhas, only four are dangerous. The most aggressive is the red-bellied piranha.

▶ **The sharp teeth of the piranha are used by forest peoples to make tools and weapons.**

There are three types of forest in the Amazon. One type is always flooded; the tree trunks grow out of water. Another type is flooded at certain times of year, when the rivers rise. These forests contain many palm trees, including the *seringueira*, or rubber tree. The third type is the dry forest, where trees can reach 200 feet (60 m) high, and their leaves form a thick barrier, or canopy, that blocks out the sunlight.

▼ **The Queen Victoria lily that grows in the flooded forests and wetlands of Brazil has the world's largest lilypads. The pads are so wide that they can support the weight of a person.**

# Wild and Wet

The wild hills and plateaus of the cerrado in the west of the country form the second largest vegetation zone in Brazil. It is a hot but dry grassland—there is not enough rain for large trees to grow. Nevertheless, the region has a biodiversity second only to the Amazon.

South of the cerrado is the Pantanal, a flat area of wetlands. The Pantanal is home to its own record-breakers: The capybara is a rodent, which makes it a distant cousin of mice and squirrels. However, the capybara grows to 4 feet (1.2 m) long and weighs 110 pounds (50 kg). The wetlands are also home to the green anaconda—the world's heaviest snake. Anacondas grow to 30 feet (9 m) and have few

▲ A farm worker shows off a yellow anaconda he has caught with his colleagues. Yellow anacondas have been hunted for their skin and are now endangered.

## PINK RIVER DOLPHIN

"Boto" is the Brazilian name for the pink river dolphin. This water mammal lives only in the rivers of the Amazon Basin. It is gray with pinkish blotches, and has a long snout filled with teeth for grabbing slippery fish. Botos live in small family groups; they are usually friendly to people and often approach swimmers. In the murky river water, the dolphins do not need good eyesight. Instead they rely on a sonar system to find prey. They produce high-pitched clicks that echo off fish, showing the dolphin where they are in the dark.

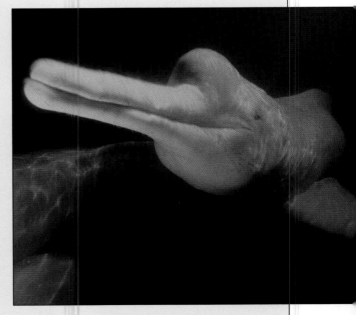

▲ The boto has a rounded "melon" on its head. This is filled with oil and is used to direct sonar calls.

enemies. The big snakes even prey on other fierce Brazilian predators—the caimans. *Caiman* is the name used for South American alligators.

# Dry Land

The *caatinga* is a much drier region of bush in the northeast. This vegetation zone is exclusively Brazilian. The sandy ground does not retain water well. Some plants, such as cactuses, hold their own water supply. Others have a wide network of roots to catch as much water as possible as it trickles through the soil. The animals of the caatinga are small species that can run and hide among the scattered plants. They include the agouti, a fast-running rodent that feeds on seeds.

The lowlands in the far south of Brazil are also too dry for forests. Instead, pampas grassland grows. As on the caatinga, animals there need to move quickly to survive. They include flightless running birds called rheas. If cornered, the tall rheas fight back with a sharp claw on the tip of each wing.

## RED TREE

Early Portuguese explorers found many brazilwood trees on the coast. Brazilwood may have been named for its red color; *brasa* was a word for glowing embers. The Portuguese named the country after the trees. Brazilwood was prized for making furniture and as a source of a red dye. Many settlers were attracted by the valuable trees. Just 50 years after the Europeans arrived in Brazil, there were no brazilwood trees within 13 miles (20 km) of the coast; by 1600 the brazilwood was an endangered species. Today the trees are protected in national parks.

▼ The brazilwood is known as *pau-brasil* by local people.

# A *New World*

**B**RAZIL WAS ADDED TO THE MAP of the world during the great European explorations in the late 15th century, led by Portugal and Spain. In 1494, the two countries agreed to divide the unexplored world between them by drawing a line down the middle of the Atlantic Ocean. Spain would take land to the west, while Portugal would seek new lands east of the line—which turned out to include the eastern bulge of Brazil. In 1500 Pedro Alvares Cabral claimed the territory for Portugal. He sailed west from Africa and landed on what is now the coast of Bahia. Fortune hunters flocked to the new land, which was originally named Vera Cruz (True Cross). Soon the name changed to Brazil for the valuable trees that grew almost everywhere.

◀ **The streets of Salvador in Bahia are filled with old-fashioned European buildings. The city was founded in 1549 as the first capital of Brazil.**

# ANCIENT CIVILIZATIONS

When Europeans reached the coast of Brazil in 1500, the country was not empty. It was home to 30 million indigenous people, or Amerindians. Until recently, it was believed that the country had been inhabited for 10,000 years. The ancestors of these first Brazilians arrived from Asia through North America. However, the remains of ancient pottery suggest that people were living in Brazil 32,000 years ago. Experts think they arrived from Pacific islands. About 300,000 Amerindians live in Brazil today. Many live in remote places, cut off from the rest of the country. There may be tribes who have never had contact with the outside world.

## Time line

This chart shows the approximate dates of events in the history of Brazil from the arrival of European explorers and settlers to the present day.

- COLOMBUS'S VOYAGE TO AMERICA
- TREATY DIVIDES UNEXPLORED WORLD BETWEEN PORTUGAL AND SPAIN
- PEDRO ALVAREZ CABRAL REACHES BRAZIL

PORTUGUESE COLONY

RIO DE JANEIRO BECOMES THE CAPITAL ●

BRASILIA BECOMES THE CAPITAL ●

BRAZILIAN EMPIRE

MILITARY DICTATORSHIP

REPUBLIC

1450   1500   1550   1600   1650   1700   1750   1800   1850   1900   1950   2000

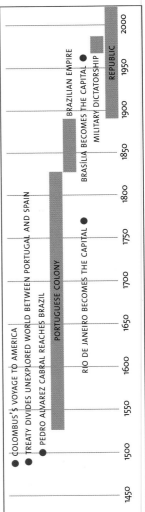

▲ Ameridian men in traditional costumes gather to demand more rights over their land. There are about 200 separate groups of indigenous peoples. Most live in reservations that cover 10 percent of Brazil.

## MAP KEY

- ☐ Hereditary Captaincies 1534
- – – – Line of the Treaty of Tordesillas
- ☐ Selected Portuguese settlements 1500s
- ● Selected present-day city

*Present-day boundaries, drainage, and place names are shown.*

miles    500
0    500
km    500
0    500

**Atlantic Ocean**

Olinda
Recife
Fortaleza
São Cristóvão
São Francisco
Salvador (Bahia)

COLONIAL BUILDINGS, pages 2–3, 24–25

Ilhéus
Porto Seguro

GOLDEN SCULPTURE, page 30

Espírito Santo

COLORFUL HOUSES, page 30 AND OLD STREETCAR, page 32

Rio de Janeiro
Santo Amaro
São Paulo
São Vicente

STATUE, page 28

CEARÁ
RIO GRANDE
ITAMARCÁ
PERNAMBUCO
BAHIA
ILHÉUS
PORTO SEGURO
Serra do Espinhaço
BRAZILIAN
HIGHLANDS
ESPÍRITO SANTO
Ouro Preto
SÃO TOMÉ
RIO DE JANEIRO
SÃO VICENTE
SANTANA

MARANHÃO
Belém
Ilha de Marajó
Tocantins
Tocantins
Araguaia

BRAZIL
Xingu
PLANALTO DO MATO GROSSO
Teles Pires
Tapajós

RAIN-FOREST MINE, page 33

UNUSUAL BUILDINGS, page 34 AND
PROTESTORS, page 35 AND
WAVING OFFICIAL, page 35

Paraná
Paraguay

WOMAN AT COMPUTER, page 31

Curitiba

PARAGUAY

Uruguay

BOLIVIA

ARGENTINA

Negro
AMAZON BASIN
Manaus
Amazon
Madeira
Guaporé

▲ A statue of Pedro Alvares Cabral in São Paulo celebrates the arrival of the Portuguese in Brazil 500 years ago.

# Like Crabs

Portugal established its first colony in Brazil in 1530. A couple of years later, the country was divided up into 14 estates called *captaincies*. Each captaincy was a strip of land stretching inland from the coast. Captaincies were awarded to noble Portuguese families, but the estates were too large to control, and few of them were prosperous. However, the modern states of Brazil still reflect these colonial boundaries.

In 1549, a governor general arrived from Portugal to rule Brazil from Salvador, the country's first capital. Colonists established sugarcane plantations and also exported coffee, diamonds, and gold to Europe.

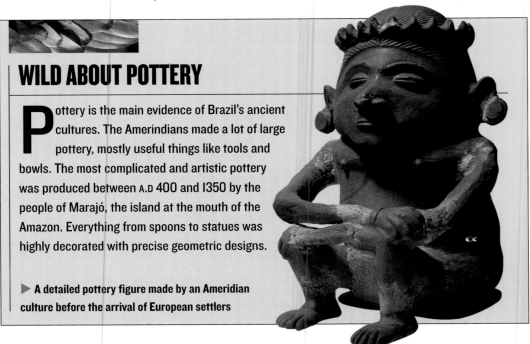

## WILD ABOUT POTTERY

Pottery is the main evidence of Brazil's ancient cultures. The Amerindians made a lot of large pottery, mostly useful things like tools and bowls. The most complicated and artistic pottery was produced between A.D 400 and 1350 by the people of Marajó, the island at the mouth of the Amazon. Everything from spoons to statues was highly decorated with precise geometric designs.

▶ A detailed pottery figure made by an Ameridian culture before the arrival of European settlers

People from West Africa were brought to Brazil to work as slaves. But for the first 100 years, few people headed far inland. Instead the colonists clung to the coast; a writer of the time said they were "like crabs."

## The Gold Rush

In the mid-1600s, colonists began to explore inland. Most of these expeditions, called *bandeiras*, were looking for Amerindian slaves and for gold. In 1690 huge reserves of gold were discovered in what is now the state of Minas Gerais.

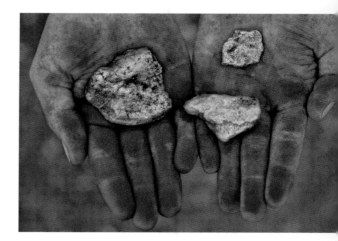

A gold rush began as people from the coastal areas and from Portugal itself headed to the gold fields in the hope of getting rich. Towns sprang up around the mines. The most important town was Ouro Preto, which means "Black Gold" for the dark soil from which the golden nuggets were dug. By 1750, Ouro Preto had a population of 80,000.

As a result of the migration, the center of the Brazilian colony shifted southeast. In 1763 the capital was moved from Salvador to Rio de Janeiro, which had become the main port for carrying gold to Europe. The gold was shipped to Portugal—but it did not remain there long. Brazilian gold ended up in London, England, where it financed the Industrial Revolution. In return, industrial goods manufactured in

▲ Three hundred years after the first Brazilian gold rush, people are still getting rich by digging for gold in Brazil. The old mines in Minas Gerais have now closed, but others have opened in the Amazon and Mato Grosso regions.

new English factories were sent to Portugal and on to Brazil.

▲ Behind the modern skyscrapers and glitzy beachfront, Rio de Janeiro has quiet streets from the 18th century, when the city was Brazil's capital.

## *Becoming a Nation*

With the wealth brought by their gold and diamond mines, the colonists started to feel more Brazilian than Portuguese. They grew unhappy that their treasure was being shipped abroad. In 1776, the United States had won its independence from Britain. In 1789 Brazilians tried to throw off Portuguese rule. The movement was crushed by the army. Then, in 1807, France invaded Portugal. The next year, the Portuguese royal family fled to Brazil, which became the seat of government. Ideas of revolution were forgotten.

## A COLONIAL GEM

**M**inas Gerais is home to many historic colonial towns. The state's name means "General Mines" in Portuguese, and the towns began life in the 1700s as rough camps filled with fortune-hunting gold miners. Within decades the camps had grown into wealthy towns with buildings that shone with gold decorations. The most ornate town is Ouro Preto. Most of its buildings were designed by the sculptor and architect Aleijadinho (1730–1814)—his name means "The Little Cripple"; his hands and feet were deformed. Aleijadinho's work is the finest example of Brazilian baroque architecture, and Ouro Preto was made a UNESCO World Heritage site in 1980.

▲ The altar of a church in Ouro Preto is decorated with one of Aleijadinho's golden sculptures.

## REMEMBERING ZUMBI

**A**bout four million Africans were brought to Brazil as slaves. For 300 years Brazil's agriculture depended on slave labor. In the 17th century, however, escaped slaves began to set up remote refuges, called *quilombos*. Some grew to be the size of cities. In the 1650s, the Palmares quilombo in northeastern Brazil was home to 30,000 people. The leader of Palmares was Africa Zumbi, who spent 60 years fighting Brazil's Portuguese leaders. However, in 1695 Zumbi was captured and beheaded. Today, Zumbi's

▲ A resident of a quilombo, or former slave refuge, in a remote part of southern Brazil takes a lesson in using the community's satellite Internet service.

execution is remembered as the National Day of Black Conscience on November 20. Many quilombos still exist and have grown into thriving communities.

## A New Kingdom

Despite the Portuguese king living in Rio de Janeiro, the colony was still set on a path to independence. In 1815, Brazil became a united kingdom with Portugal. When the king returned to Portugal in 1821, he left his son Pedro in Brazil with the title of Viceroy. The prince broke with Portugal and proclaimed Brazil an independent country on September 7, 1822.

The Spanish colonies in South and Central America ended up as 18 different countries after bitter wars. Brazil avoided such violence. It came about by negotiation, which ensured that it did not break apart. That is one reason it remains the largest and most powerful country on the continent.

Pedro I ruled Brazil as an empire until 1831, when he gave up his throne to return to Portugal. He was replaced by his son. Pedro II was only a teenager when he took the throne, but his 49-year reign established Brazil as a modern country. Health and welfare programs were introduced, the first railroads were built, and slavery was slowly reduced.

## Republican Rebellion

Despite the emperor's success, wars with Uruguay, Argentina, and Paraguay between 1851 and 1870 weakened his power. In 1888 slavery was finally abolished. The next year, military leaders and landowners unhappy about abolition forced Pedro II to leave the country.

Brazil became a federal republic—as it remains today. The armed forces soon became very powerful: The two first presidents were generals. Even recently, the army has been influential in Brazil's government.

▲ Rio de Janeiro had a network of streetcars installed in the I860s during the modernization by Pedro II. Today a handful of cars still run.

## Crisis Management

During the world economic crisis that followed the Wall Street Crash of 1929, the price of coffee—Brazil's chief export—fell so low that the country ran out of money. The government was in chaos until Getúlio Vargas took power. Vargas's rule, from 1930 to 1945, was a period of huge change for Brazil. The country could not afford to buy many goods from abroad, so factories were built to make them. Although Vargas had not been elected, many of his reforms made life better for ordinary Brazilians.

When World War II broke out in 1939, Vargas kept Brazil neutral. However, in 1941 the United States entered the war. Vargas allowed U.S. bombers and supply planes to be based in the Brazilian bulge, which was only a short flight from Africa and southern Europe. In August 1942, Brazil joined the war on the same side as the United States, Britain, and France.

## *Growing Pains*

The next civilian president of Brazil was Juscelino Kubitschek, who was elected in 1955. Kubitschek was ambitious: He named his economic plan "Fifty

▲ Juscelino Kubitschek (right) stands beside U.S. President Dwight Eisenhower (left) in the late 1950s.

▼ Brazil's economic boom of the 1950s and '60s was hard to control, as can be seen in this unregulated gold mine dug in the rain forest.

# A CAPITAL ON THE MOVE

The idea of moving the capital of Brazil from Rio to the center of the country was first suggested in the 19th century. Planners hoped that a new inland city would attract people away from the crowded coasts and would also separate the political power from Brazil's economic center. The time for the move came during the boom of the 1950s. The new capital Brasília was built as an ultra-modern city designed by the architect Oscar Niemeyer and President Juscelino Kubitschek himself. Brasília was completed in five years and declared the capital in 1960. At first the unusual buildings made the city seem strange and it took a few years to attract many settlers. Today, Brasília has a population of 2.5 million people, who love their unique city. Brasília was made a UNESCO World Heritage site in 1987.

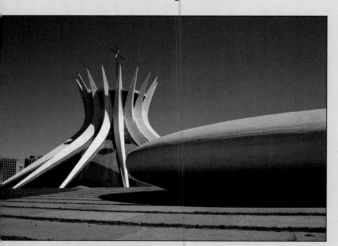

▲ Like many of the buildings in the city, Brasília's Cathedral Metropolitiana does not follow a traditional shape.

Years of Progress in Five." During his four years of office, industrial output grew by an astonishing 80 percent. Kubitschek also built a new capital city, Brasília.

João Goulart replaced Kubitschek as president in 1961. He had socialist ideas—he planned to take control of Brazil's land and natural resources and have them managed by the government on behalf of all the people. In 1964, wealthy landowners and military leaders who feared that they would lose out threw Goulart out of office. The United States, which was nervous about communists running Brazil, helped the rebels take power.

## Dictatorship

Brazil was ruled by military dictators for the next 21 years. They were often incompetent and corrupt. Instead of developing new industries, the government borrowed money from abroad to pay for running the country. Brazil's environment began to suffer, as poor people were relocated to the Amazon to clear the land for farms. The military crushed any protests, and people—even elected politicians—were afraid to criticize the government for fear that they would be put into prison.

## *Democracy Regained*

By the early 1980s things had gotten so bad that people rose up against the government. A movement called *Diretas Já*—meaning "Elections Now"—became very popular. Millions of Brazilians demonstrated in the streets. The military government finally resigned in 1985.

A caretaker government took over until 1989, when Fernando Collor was elected president. However, after two years, Collor was thrown out for corruption. The next election in 1994 was more successful. Fernando Henrique Cardoso, one of the leaders of Diretas Já, won easily. He implemented the *Plano Real*—a financial plan to reorganize Brazil's economy so it could compete with other countries. Cardoso was re-elected in 1998. The Plano Real helped establish Brazil as a country with a great future.

▲ A crowd gathers to demand democracy in Brasilia in 1985.

▼ President Henrique Cardoso gives a thumbs up to the crowd during the annual Independence Day parade.

# A *Melting Pot*

**W**HEN EUROPE WAS BEING devastated by wars in the early 20th century, many Europeans looked to Brazil as an idealized paradise where people of all races lived in harmony and peace. All Brazilians are descended from three ethnic groups: the Amerindians, European settlers—mainly from Portugal—and Africans forcibly shipped there as slaves. Since the beginning, these groups have been mixing. The Portuguese settlers, who were mostly young men seeking a new life, married Amerindian women. Their children were called *mamelucos*. A few years later, when Africans began to arrive, there was more integration: *Cafusos* had Amerindian and African parents. The children of Europeans and Africans were called *mulattoes*.

◀ **The streets of São Paulo bustle with Brazilians of all races. Most of their ancestors arrived in the country during the last 500 years.**

# CROWDED CITIES

The number of Brazilians has tripled in 50 years, making the population the fifth largest in the world. Much of the country is almost empty of people, but the life of most Brazilians is a crowded one. Three-quarters of them live in the south in an area that covers only 18 percent of the country. Four out of five Brazilians are city dwellers, mostly living along the coast. Brazil's cities are still growing as people move from the rural north. The population increase is also due to better health care, so fewer people die young. Brazil has become a country of young people: 68 percent of its citizens are under 60 years old.

▲ Belo Horizonte, Brazil's third largest city, is gradually expanding into the surrounding countryside.

| 1950 / 54 million | 1970 / 96 million |
|---|---|
| 36% urban / 64% rural | 56% urban / 44% rural |

| 1990 / 149 million | 2005 / 186 million |
|---|---|
| 75% urban / 25% rural | 84% urban / 16% rural |

# Common Portuguese Phrases

There are about 180 languages spoken by Brazil's Amerindian tribes, but everyone else speaks Portuguese. Here are a few Portuguese words and phrases you might use in Brazil. Give them a try:

| | |
|---|---|
| How do you do? | Como vai você? |
| Hello | Olá, Alô (on the telephone) |
| Good morning | Bom dia |
| Good afternoon | Boa tarde |
| Good evening | Boa noite |
| Good bye | Adeus |
| Please | Por favor |
| Thank you | Obrigado (said by men) |
| | Obrigada (said by women) |
| Yes | Sim |
| No | Não |
| My name is... | Meu nome é... |
| Sorry | Desculpe |

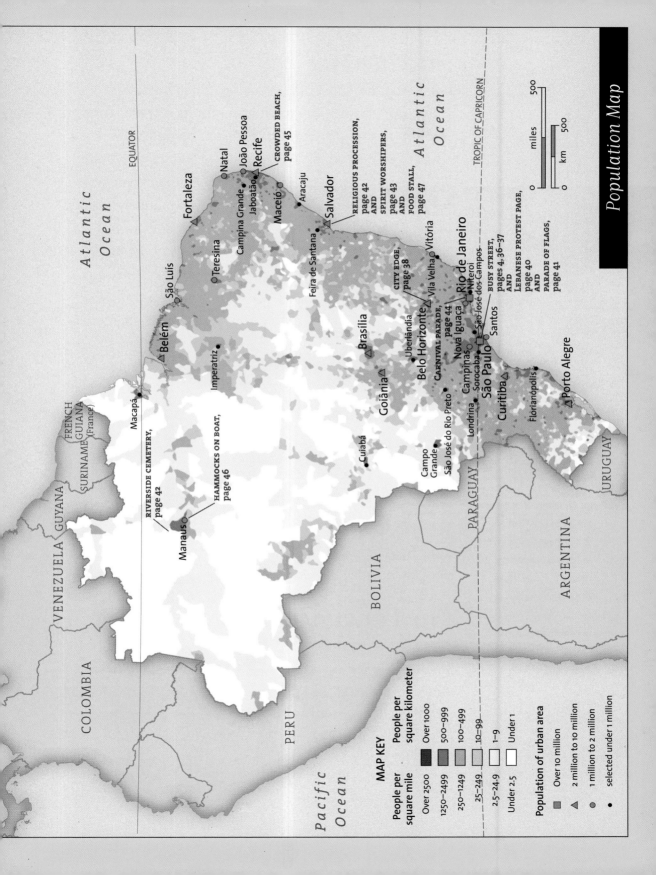

# Population Map

COLOMBIA

VENEZUELA

GUYANA

SURINAME

FRENCH GUIANA (France)

*Atlantic Ocean*

EQUATOR

Macapá

Belém

São Luís

Fortaleza

Natal

João Pessoa

Jaboatão

Campina Grande

Recife

**CROWDED BEACH,**
page 45

Maceió

Aracaju

Teresina

Salvador

**RELIGIOUS PROCESSION,**
page 42
AND
**SPIRIT WORSHIPERS,**
page 43
AND
**FOOD STALL,**
page 47

Feira de Santana

*Atlantic Ocean*

Manaus

**RIVERSIDE CEMETERY,**
page 42

**HAMMOCKS ON BOAT,**
page 46

Imperatriz

PERU

Cuiabá

Brasília

Goiânia

Uberlândia

Belo Horizonte

**CITY EDGE,**
page 38

Vila Velha

Vitória

**CARNIVAL PARADE,**
page 44

Niterói

Rio de Janeiro

São José dos Campos

**BUSY STREET,**
pages 4, 36–37
AND
**LEBANESE PROTEST, page,**
page 40
AND
**PARADE OF FLAGS,**
page 41

BOLIVIA

Campo Grande

São José do Rio Preto

Londrina

Nova Iguaçu

Campinas

Sorocaba

São Paulo

Santos

PARAGUAY

Curitiba

Florianópolis

Porto Alegre

ARGENTINA

URUGUAY

TROPIC OF CAPRICORN

*Pacific Ocean*

## MAP KEY

### People per square mile / People per square kilometer

| People per square mile | People per square kilometer |
| --- | --- |
| Over 2500 | Over 1000 |
| 1250–2499 | 500–999 |
| 250–1249 | 100–499 |
| 25–249 | 10–99 |
| 2.5–24.9 | 1–9 |
| Under 2.5 | Under 1 |

### Population of urban area

- ◼ Over 10 million
- ▲ 2 million to 10 million
- ● 1 million to 2 million
- • selected under 1 million

miles 0 ———— 500

km 0 ———— 500

## Into the Mix

Brazil's cultural and racial mix has received several shake-ups as later waves of immigrants arrived from Europe. In the 19th century, people came to the country to take up the jobs that had previously been filled by slaves from Africa. Germans and Swiss settled in the south of Brazil. However, Portugal remained the most important source of arrivals in Brazil, followed by Italy and Spain. In the first half of the 20th century, people escaping turmoil in Central and Eastern Europe arrived, including many Jews. There has also been a migration from Japan, while Christian Arabs came from Syria and Lebanon. Whatever their background, people in Brazil all feel they are Brazilians.

▲ Lebanese Brazilians gather in São Paolo in 2006 to protest conflict between Lebanon and its neighbor, Israel. Many Brazilian immigrants remain closely interested in their home countries.

## One Language, Many Gods

One of the main things that unites Brazilians is their language—Portuguese. Only Amerindians living in very remote regions speak other languages. Brazilians are the only Latin Americans who do not speak Spanish. Brazilian Portuguese has no regional accents or dialects, but it does include many Amerindian words for the names of fruits and plants. African words for food and musical instruments are also part of the language.

Brazil has no official religion and different faiths are sometimes mixed together. Brazilian people are often relaxed about their beliefs. Some attend worship for two or three different religions.

Three-quarters of the people are Roman Catholics. The Catholic Church in Brazil was at the forefront of opposing military rule in 1970s and 1980s. The second largest group are the Protestants, who represent 15 percent of the population.

Other people follow religions that orginated in Africa, such as Candomblé and Umbanda. These faiths were brought by the slaves and have become combined with Amerindian beliefs and Catholic saints. There are also followers of Spiritism, who believe that the dead can communicate with the living through a special person called a medium.

# NATIONAL HOLIDAYS

**B**razilians enjoy the holidays. The biggest celebration is Carnival, which is a party linked to the Christian calendar. It is the last feast before Easter and takes place during the three days before Ash Wednesday. There are three national days in Brazil. One commemorates the first attempt at independence in 1789—it is celebrated in the name of the revolutionary leader, Tiradentes. Independence Day celebrates the foundation of the nation in 1822, while the Proclamation of the Republic Day remembers the creation of the first government a few months later. Only Independence Day is celebrated publicly with parades (below).

| | |
|---|---|
| **JANUARY 1:** | New Year's Day |
| **FEBRUARY/MARCH:** | Carnival |
| **MARCH/APRIL:** | Good Friday / Easter Sunday |
| **APRIL 21:** | Tiradentes Day |
| **MAY 1:** | Labor Day |
| **MAY/JUNE:** | Corpus Christi |
| **SEPTEMBER 7:** | Independence Day |
| **OCTOBER 12:** | *Nossa Senhora Aparecida* (Brazil's Patron Saint) |
| **NOVEMBER 2:** | All Soul's Day |
| **NOVEMBER 15:** | Proclamation of the Republic Day |
| **NOVEMBER 20:** | National Day of Black Conscience |
| **DECEMBER 25:** | Christmas Day |

# Holy Rites

As a mainly Catholic country, Brazil's major holidays are Christian events. In June the feast of St. Anthony, John, and Peter is celebrated at *Festa Juanina*—a mock wedding party with bonfires and people dancing in costumes.

The patron saint of Brazil is Our Lady of Aparecida, who is represented by a small statue of the Virgin Mary in a church in the city of Aparecida, near São Paulo. A similar statue is involved in the Cirio de Nazaré festival held in Belém every October. The statue is carried across the Amazon followed by hundreds of small boats.

▲ **Catholic women parade through the historic streets of Salvador.**

▼ **Crosses mark graves in a cemetery on a beach beside the Rio Negro in the heart of the rain forest.**

The main Christmas event is a lavish family meal on Christmas Eve. New Year's Eve is celebrated with fireworks displays. The display on Copacabana Beach in Rio de Janeiro attracts thousands of spectators from all over the world. Some come dressed in white and make offerings to Iemanjá, the goddess of the sea.

## SPIRITS AND SAINTS

About two million Brazilians follow Candomblé, a religion influenced by African culture. It involves rituals, music, and dances that were brought to Brazil by enslaved people. Because slaves were not allowed to practice their own religion, they mixed their spirits, or *orixas*, with the Catholic saints of their Portuguese masters. For instance Oxala, the god of the harvest, is also Jesus, and Iemanjá, goddess of the sea, is the Virgin Mary.

▲ Followers of Candomblé attempt to contact spirits.

## *Telling Stories*

Children's stories tell about the history of Brazil in a way that blends the country's many cultures. Monteiro Lobato wrote many kids' favorites in the early 20th century. His characters live on a farm called the *Sito do Pica-Pau Amarelo* (Yellow Woodpecker Ranch). Their adventures lead them to meet many characters from Brazilian folklore, such as Saci Pererê—a one-legged elf. Brazil's most famous comic strips are by Mauricio de Sousa. They tell lively stories about three very different types of Brazilian children. In *Turma da*

# THE BIGGEST PARTY ON EARTH

Brazil's Carnival is the most famous party in the world. For three days in February and March, Brazilians sing and dance in a festival that has its roots in ancient celebrations of spring. These were later incorporated into the Christian feast before Lent. (Lent is the 40 days before Easter during which Christians give up luxuries.) In Europe, people traditionally danced in the streets wearing masks. In Portugal, people also threw water and flour over the dancers. These traditions traveled to Brazil, and the streets ran riot with people wearing colorful clothes and playing pranks. In the mid-19th century, wild street parties were gradually replaced by organized parades. Today's Carnival has everything: frenzied parties, traditional costume balls, and spectacular parades by members of the city's many samba dance schools. Rio's samba parades are the most famous part of Carnival. Each school of samba has about 5,000 members, mostly ordinary people from the suburbs, but celebrities are also invited to join in. The samba shows often combine dance with a political or social theme.

▲ The colors and floats of the samba parades are the highlights of the Rio Carnival.

*Monica*, the children live in the city; in *Chico Bento* they live on a farm; and *Papa Capim* is about young Amerindians living in the forest.

## Learning in Brazil

It is compulsory for all children to attend school from the age of 7 to 14. However, Brazil still has a high illiteracy rate: 14 percent of the population—26 million people—cannot read or write. Some families are too poor to send their children to school. These children have to start work at about age 10 or stay at home to look after smaller children so that their parents can work.

Beginning around the age of 15, children can attend secondary school for three years, but only 40 percent of the age group enrolls for school. Secondary schooling ends at 18. Both public and private universities have an entrance exam and it is very difficult to get in.

## *Brasilidade*

All forms of Brazilian culture are sometimes grouped together under the label Brasilidade. The main contributions of Brasilidade are modern architecture, such as the buildings of Brasília, and music.

▲ Brazil is blessed with miles of sandy beaches, and many Brazilians spend their free time relaxing and playing sports by the sea.

## THE WORLD AT HIS FEET

Brazilians are soccer crazy and their country produced the greatest player ever: Edson Arantes Nascimento, better known as Pelé. After helping Brazil win the 1958 World Cup at the age of just 17, Pelé won a worldwide following. In 1967 a ceasefire was declared during the civil war in Nigeria so people could watch Pelé play in the capital. Pelé scored 1,280 goals in 1,360 games, more than any other player. Since retiring he has starred in movies and served as Brazil's sports minister.

▲ Pelé makes his trademark overhead kick.

▲ Gilberto Gil has been one of Brazil's favorite pop singers since his career began in the 1960s. Gil has also been a political activist: In 2003 he was appointed as Brazil's culture minister.

Brazilian music blends Amerindian reed flutes with Portuguese guitars and African drum rhythms. There have been music schools in the country since the 17th century, when religious music was played throughout the colony.

Art and music were given a boost in the early 19th century when the Portuguese royal family ruled from Brazil. The late-19th century composer Carlos Gomes wrote Italian-style operas but with Brazilian themes, such as *O Guarani*. In the 20th century, Heitor Villa-Lobos brought Brazilian folk melodies and rhythms to classical music.

Brazil's popular music developed alongside classical music. It united European instruments with new rhythms to make dance music such as *maxixe*, *batuque*, *choro*, *frevo*, *baião*, and samba. Samba was created in the 20th century and has became the most famous. "Aquarela do Brazil," an early samba by Ari

## THE FLOATING BIRDCAGE

Gaiola, meaning birdcage, is the name given to the slow passenger boats that transport people on the Amazon River. The name comes from the bars along the sides of their open decks and because travelers often sing songs to pass the time.

▲ Gaiola passengers spend the long journeys in hammocks strung across the boat.

Barroso usually known simply as "Brazil," is played worldwide today. In the 1950s Tom Jobim and João Gilberto created bossa nova, a type of jazz. "The Girl from Ipanema" is one of the most famous songs in the world—Ipanema is a district of Rio de Janeiro.

## Dishing Up

Different areas of Brazil are known for growing certain foods, and each region has its own distinct style of cooking. Cassava is a staple food everywhere. It is used to make flat breads, called *tapioca*; *pão-de-queijo*, or cheese bread; and moist, spicy dumplings called *farofa*. Beans are another basic food, prepared in stews with different meats and vegetables. The most popular stew is called *feijoada*—from the word *feijão* for "beans."

▲ A street vendor in Salvador has a range of snacks to offer. The spicy snacks are called *salgadinhos*; the sweet ones are *docinhos*.

With their large rivers and long coast, Brazilians eat a lot of fish and shellfish. They also love *churrasco*, or barbecue. Churrasco originated in the cattle country to the south, but is enjoyed all over the country. The national drink, besides fresh fruit juices, is *guaraná*—a sparkling soft drink made from the berries of the guaraná, a plant native to the Amazon.

# Prepared
## for
# Greatness

UNTIL RECENTLY, BRAZIL WAS not one of the world's developed economies. Thanks to its wealth of natural resources, it is now set to take its place as a leading economic power. While the rich nations of North America and Europe struggle with the problems of global climate change, and search for ways of reducing how much carbon dioxide they produce, Brazil is already far ahead of them. Its enormous rivers are used to generate clean electricity. Brazil does have oil fields along its coast, but the country also has a more ecological source of fuel. Sugarcane produces ethanol, or alcohol, that can be used in place of gasoline. Unlike gasoline, the supply of sugarcane will never run out. Cars in Brazil run on biodiesel—a mixture of ethanol and gasoline.

◀ Truckloads of sugarcane arrive at an ethanol plant, where the sugar is turned into ethanol in a process similar to the one used to make alcoholic drinks.

# MAINTAINING DEMOCRACY

**B**razil has struggled with democracy in its recent history. Full democracy returned in 1985, when a military government was peacefully removed. However, it took another 10 years before Brazilian politics and the economy became stable again.

Brazil is a federal republic of 26 *estados*, or states. The states are divided into municipalities. Each state has a governor, and the municipalities have elected mayors. State boundaries have developed over the centuries and many are largely unchanged since the colonial period. Brasília, where the national government is based, is located in the separate Federal District.

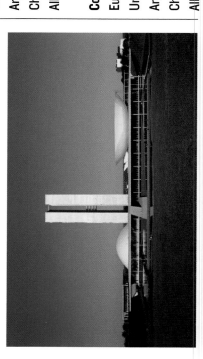

▲ **The Palace of Congress in Brasília is a unique government building. The Senate sits inside the dome, while the lower House of Deputies gathers in the upturned hemisphere.**

# Trading Partners

**T**he European Union (EU) has recently replaced the United States as Brazil's main trading partner. Germany is the main partner within the EU. Brazil joined the World Trade Organization in 1995 so it could make trading agreements with more developing countries. Brazil trades with other South American countries (except French Guiana) through UNASUL (Union of South American Nations). UNASUL was created in 2004 to make the continent a free-trade area. Brazil's main exports are meat, coffee, vehicles, and metals. It imports chemicals and electronics.

| Country | Percent Brazil exports |
|---|---|
| European Union | 22.1% |
| United States | 18.0% |
| Argentina | 8.5% |
| China | 6.1% |
| All others combined | 45.3% |

| Country | Percent Brazil imports |
|---|---|
| European Union | 22.0% |
| United States | 16.3% |
| Argentina | 8.8% |
| China | 8.7% |
| All others combined | 44.2% |

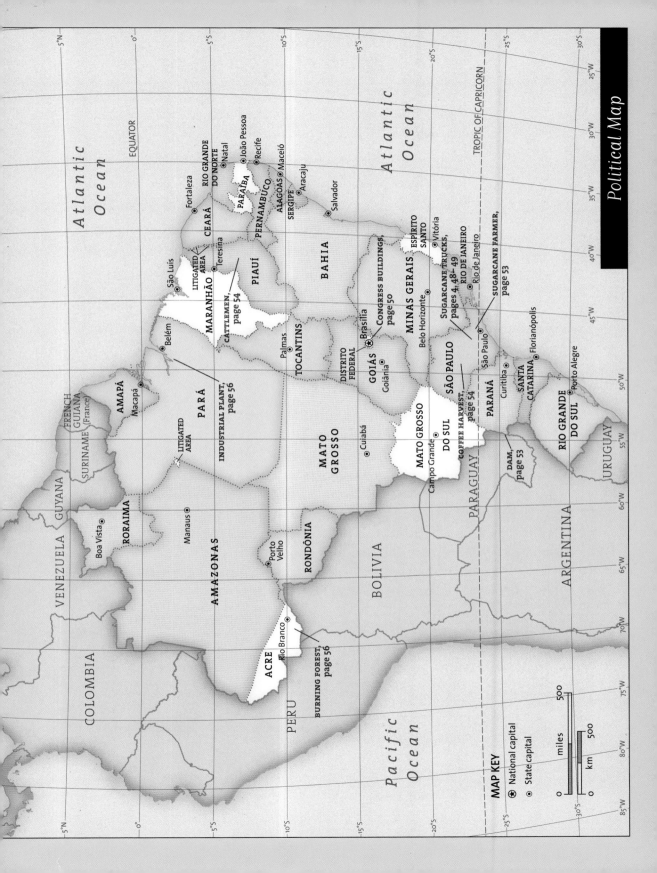

Political Map

Atlantic Ocean

EQUATOR

TROPIC OF CAPRICORN

Atlantic Ocean

Pacific Ocean

COLOMBIA

VENEZUELA

GUYANA

SURINAME

FRENCH GUIANA (France)

PERU

BOLIVIA

PARAGUAY

ARGENTINA

URUGUAY

Boa Vista

RORAIMA

AMAZONAS

Manaus

Porto Velho

RONDÔNIA

ACRE
Rio Branco

BURNING FOREST, page 56

AMAPÁ
Macapá

Belém

LITIGATED AREA

INDUSTRIAL PLANT, page 56

PARÁ

LITIGATED AREA

São Luís

MARANHÃO

Teresina

PIAUÍ

CATTLEMEN, page 54

Fortaleza

CEARÁ

RIO GRANDE DO NORTE
Natal

PARAÍBA
João Pessoa

PERNAMBUCO
Recife

ALAGOAS
Maceió

SERGIPE
Aracaju

BAHIA

Salvador

MATO GROSSO

Cuiabá

TOCANTINS

Palmas

DISTRITO FEDERAL
Brasília

GOIÁS
Goiânia

CONGRESS BUILDINGS, page 50

MINAS GERAIS

Belo Horizonte

ESPÍRITO SANTO
Vitória

SUGARCANE TRUCKS, pages 4, 48–49

RIO DE JANEIRO
Rio de Janeiro

SUGARCANE FARMER, page 53

MATO GROSSO DO SUL

Campo Grande

COFFEE HARVEST, page 54

SÃO PAULO
São Paulo

PARANÁ
Curitiba

DAM, page 53

SANTA CATARINA
Florianópolis

RIO GRANDE DO SUL
Porto Alegre

MAP KEY

⊛ National capital
⊙ State capital

miles 0        500

km 0        500

## The Wealth of the Nation

Gross domestic product, or GDP, is the value of everything a country produces in a year. Brazil's GDP is the 10th largest in the world. But when it is divided up among the country's very large population—to produce what economists call the GDP per capita—Brazil tumbles down the world ranking to 95th. This reflects the fact that Brazil is a very unequal society. The poorest 20 percent of the population have only 3 percent of the country's income. The richest 20 percent own 65 percent of the wealth. There are also

# HOW THE GOVERNMENT WORKS

The head of state of Brazil is the president. He or she is the leader of the government and appoints a cabinet of ministers, who run the country. The president is elected by the people for a 4-year period and can be re-elected only once. The vice president is elected at the same time. Brazil's legislature, or law-making body, is called the National Congress. It is divided into two parts, or chambers. The Chamber of Deputies has 513 members elected from around the country every 4 years. The Federal Senate has 81 members who sit for 8 years at a time. Both chambers and the president can suggest new laws. Brazil's highest court is the Supreme Federal Tribunal. This has 11 judges who are appointed for life by the president. The court's role is to ensure that new laws are legal under Brazil's constitution. The Superior Tribunal of Justice ensures that all states are applying the laws in the same way.

| GOVERNMENT | | |
|---|---|---|
| EXECUTIVE | LEGISLATIVE | JUDICIARY |
| PRESIDENT | FEDERAL SENATE (81 MEMBERS) | SUPREME FEDERAL TRIBUNAL |
| CABINET OF MINISTERS | CHAMBER OF DEPUTIES (513 MEMBERS) | SUPERIOR TRIBUNAL OF JUSTICE |

wide variations in wealth and living standards across the country. The wealthiest people live in the southeast, which produces more than half of the country's GDP.

## Bumper Crops

Brazil has many different soils and climates, so it can produce a great variety of crops. The country has been a major producer of sugarcane since the 16th century. Its forests were also tapped for natural rubber made with latex (sticky sap) from under the bark of certain trees. In the 19th century, coffee, cocoa beans, and cotton were added to the list.

Brazil's farms have now been modernized so the country can compete with other food producers. Brazil now grows a much wider range of crops, including soybeans, rice, corn, and wheat. The tropical regions grow valuable fruits such as bananas, avocados, pineapples, oranges, and lemons. Cooler areas produce apples and grapes. Although most of the world's rubber is now made from crude oil, natural latex, waxes, and fibers are still produced. They can be harvested from the forests but are also cultivated on plantations.

▲ The Itaipu Dam across the Parana River is Brazil's largest power plant.

▼ Sugarcane crops tower above a farmer on a vast plantation near São Paulo.

▲ Coffee berries are raked out to dry in the sun at a plantation in the south of Brazil.

Brazil's huge grasslands are ideal for raising animals, especially cows for beef. However, Brazil's tropical climate means that cattle are prone to diseases spread by flies and other bugs.

## An Awful Lot of Coffee

"The Coffee Song" made famous by U.S singer Frank Sinatra contains the line, "They've got an awful lot of coffee in Brazil." The song is right: Brazil is the world's largest producer. The crop was introduced by the Portuguese in 1727. By the 1900s Brazil produced 80 percent of the world's supply. The state of São

▼ Cattlemen tend their herd on the dry grassland of northeastern Brazil.

# INDUSTRY

**B**razil is the most highly industrialized nation in South America. Heavy industry accounts for 38 percent of the economy. The main industries are chemical plants, steel production, and the manufacture of aircraft and motor vehicles. Brazil is a producer of metals, such as iron, manganese, nickel, aluminum, and uranium. Major industrial areas are located in the southeast and southern regions, with the São Paulo region having the highest concentration of industries.

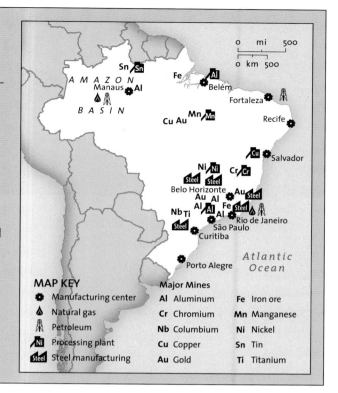

MAP KEY

- ✿ Manufacturing center
- ⛰ Natural gas
- 🗼 Petroleum
- Ni Processing plant
- Steel Steel manufacturing

Major Mines

| | |
|---|---|
| **Al** Aluminum | **Fe** Iron ore |
| **Cr** Chromium | **Mn** Manganese |
| **Nb** Columbium | **Ni** Nickel |
| **Cu** Copper | **Sn** Tin |
| **Au** Gold | **Ti** Titanium |

Paulo has the best climate and soil conditions for growing coffee, which helped make it Brazil's wealthiest region. Coffee sales financed the industrialization of the state. Brazil is still the largest coffee producer today, accounting for a quarter of the global total.

## Made in Brazil

Until the 1950s Brazil's economy was based on the export of food and raw materials. Since then manufacturing and service industries have grown quickly. Industrialization started after World War II. The first steel mill, Volta Redonda, was built in the 1940s

▲ This huge aluminum plant is located near Belém at the mouth of the Amazon. The Tocatins River generates electricity for the plant.

and made other industries possible. Car plants were introduced in the 1950s. The military government invested in similar industries but few were successful.

In the 1990s government factories were sold to private companies, and Brazil's industry has recovered. One of the most remarkable is the aircraft industry. It is just 30 years old, but now supplies small aircraft to many countries. Brazilians claim that their countryman Santos Dumont made the first self-powered flight in 1906. They argue that the Wright Brothers' celebrated 1903 flight did not count because the aircraft was catapulted into the air.

## RUBBER HERO

Chico Mendes (1944–1988) was a Brazilian rubber-tapper who became a famous environmental campaigner. He fought against logging and land clearance in the Amazon forest. Mendes organized the rubber tappers into a union that campaigned to save the forests for making rubber and to protect its wildlife. In 1988, Mendes was murdered by ranchers who wanted to clear his land. The culprits were caught, and the forest was later made into the Chico Mendes Reserve.

▲ Forest trees are burned to make way for a ranch.

## RAGS TO RICHES

When Luiz Inacio Lula da Silva was elected president in 2002, he became Brazil's first president from humble beginnings. Lula da Silva, known simply as Lula, had a remarkable rise to power. He came from a poor, illiterate family, and had little schooling. He managed to find a job in a factory in São Paulo, but lost his left index finger in a press when he was 19 years old. Lula has said that it was the bad treatment he received after this accident that turned him into a campaigner for workers' rights. He became a trade union leader before founding *Partido dos Trabalhadores* (The Workers' Party). In 1986 he won a seat in Congress. Lula ran for president four times before his 2002 election victory. His success continued while he was in office—Lula was re-elected for a second term in 2006.

▲ Luiz Inacio Lula da Silva gives his trademark "L" sign during the 2002 election campaign.

# The Country of the Future

Brazil could become one of the world's wealthiest nations in the coming decades. However, it also has a heavy responsibility to share its wealth with all of its people, while maintaining its remarkable wildlife.

▼ A mechanic works inside the body of an aircraft.

Brazil has won the soccer World Cup more than any other country—five times. The country last hosted the tournament in 1950, a time of great hope for the future. In 2014, Brazil hosts the finals again—and Brazilians have a lot to look forward to once more.

# Add a Little Extra to Your Country Report!

I f you are assigned to write a report about Brazil, you'll want to include basic information about the country, of course. The Fast Facts chart on page 8 will give you a good start. The rest of the book will give you the details you need to create a full and up-to-date paper or PowerPoint presentation. But what can you do to make your report more fun than anyone else's? If you use your imagination and dig a bit deeper into some of the topics introduced in this book, you're sure to come up with information that will make your report unique!

## >Flag

Perhaps you could explain the history of Brazil's flag, and the meanings of its colors and symbols. Go to **www.crwflags.com/fotw/flags** for more information.

## >National Anthem

How about downloading Brazil's national anthem, and playing it for your class? At **www.nationalanthems.info** you'll find what you need, including the words to the anthem, plus sheet music for it. Simply pick "B" and then "Brazil" from the list on the left-hand side of the screen, and you're on your way.

## >Time Difference

If you want to understand the time difference between Brazil and where you are, this Web site can help: **www.worldtimeserver.com**. Just pick "Brazil" from the list on the left. If you called someone in Brazil right now, would you wake them up from their sleep?

## >*Currency*

Another Web site will convert your money into reals, the currency used in Brazil. You'll want to know how much money to bring if you're ever lucky enough to travel to Brazil: **www.xe.com/ucc**.

## >*Weather*

Why not check the current weather in Brazil? It's easy—go to **www.weather.com** to find out if it's sunny or cloudy, warm or cold in Brazil right now! Pick "World" from the headings at the top of the page. Then search for Brazil. Click on any city. Be sure to click on the tabs below the weather report for Sunrise/Sunset information, Weather Watch, and Business Travel Outlook, too. Scroll down the page for the 36-hour Forecast and a satellite weather map. Compare your weather to the weather in the Brazilian city you chose. Is this a good season, weather-wise, for a person to travel to Brazil?

## >*Miscellaneous*

Still want more information? Simply go to National Geographic's World Atlas for Young Explorers at **http://www.nationalgeographic.com/kids-world.atlas**. It will help you find maps, photos, music, games, and other features that you can use to jazz up your report.

# Glossary

**Amerindian** a native American person living in South America. The word is formed from American Indian, a more old-fashioned name for this ethnic group.

**Climate** the average weather of a certain place at different times of year.

**Colony** a region that is ruled by a nation located somewhere else in the world. Settlers from that distant country take the land from the region's original inhabitants.

**Communism** a system of government where a single political party rules a country with the job of ensuring that wealth is shared equally among all the people in the country.

**Culture** a collection of beliefs, traditions, and styles that belongs to people living in a certain part of the world.

**Democracy** a country that is ruled by a government chosen by all its people through elections.

**Dictator** a leader who has complete control over a country and does not have to be elected or re-elected to office regularly. Dictators are often cruel and corrupt.

**Economy** the system by which a country creates wealth through making and trading in products.

**Ethnic** describing a section of a country's population with members that share a common ancestry or background.

**Exported** transported and sold outside the country of origin.

**Hemisphere** one half of a sphere, or globe; Brazil's congress buildings are this shape.

**Imported** brought into the country from abroad.

**Natural resources** naturally occurring materials and substances that can be collected and sold. Natural resources include oil, metals, or lumber.

**Neutral** not taking sides; during wars neutral countries do not have any allies, or friendly nations, but they also have no enemies.

**Patron saint** a country's main saint.

**Plateau** an area of land that is high but flat.

**Republic** a country that is ruled by an elected head of state, such as a president.

**Roman Catholic** a Christian who follows a branch of the religion based in Rome, Italy.

**Slum** a district of a city where the poorest communities live in badly built homes without the water, power, and sewerage services of more wealthy areas.

**Socialist** a person who believes in a political system in which the government manages a country's industries on behalf of all its people; a less extreme version of communism.

**Sonar** a system for detecting objects using pulses of sound that echo off surfaces in the area; the timing of the echoes is used to figure out where objects are.

**Species** a type of organism; animals or plants in the same species look similar and can only breed successfully among themselves.

**Sustainable** something that can continue forever without needing to be mended, added to, or running out. Sustainable development is building factories or setting up farms in a way that will not damage the environment.

# Bibliography

Freland, François-Xavier. *We Live in Brazil*. New York, NY: Abrams Books for Young Readers, 2007.

Scoones, Simon. *Focus on Brazil*. Milwaukee, WI: World Almanac Library, 2007.

Shields, Charles J. *Brazil*. Philadelphia, PA: Mason Crest Publishers, 2004.

http://www.braziltourism.org/ (official Web site of Brazilian Tourism Office)

http://news.bbc.co.uk/1/hi/world/americas/country_profiles/1227110.stm (general information)

# Further Information

## NATIONAL GEOGRAPHIC Articles

Wallace, Scott. "Last of the Amazon." NATIONAL GEOGRAPHIC (January 2007): 40–71.

## Web sites to explore

More fast facts about Brazil, from the CIA (Central Intelligence Agency): https://www.cia.gov/library/publications/the-world-factbook/geos/br.html

Brasília is one of the newest capital cities in the world. It did not exist 100 years ago. It was built to show off Brazil as a modern country. It has many examples of architecture in the modernist style. Despite the name of this style, the buildings look a little old-fashioned today. Nevertheless Brasília is still a handsome city, unlike any other in the world. Take a look at pictures of Brazil's capital at this site: http://www.aboutbrasilia.com/

Samba is Brazil's music. Its name comes from a West African word meaning "praying to spirits." Samba is music for dancing, and the biggest samba parties in the world are held at the Rio Carnival each year. But samba is also fun to listen to. See what you think at: http://music.calabash music.com/world/Samba

## See, hear

There are many ways to get a taste of life in Brazil, such as movies and music. You might be able to locate these:

*Ronaldinho Gaucho*
A comic strip about Ronaldinho, one of the star players in Brazil's national soccer team. The strip is produced by Brazil's master cartoonist Mauricio de Sousa. It tells the story of Ronaldinho, who is known for his large front teeth and ponytail hairstyle, as a child with his soccer-crazy buddies. Other characters include Ronaldinho's brother Asis, sister Daisy, and number-one fan Diego. You can follow this daily strip at: http://www.uclick.com/client/zzz/ron/

*House of Sand (2006)*
An award-winning film made in the desert region of northeastern Brazil. Set in 1910, a small family moves there to start a farm. Soon the white settlers realize they are not alone: A quilombo, or ex-slave colony, is located nearby. The father goes mad and dies leaving his wife and daughter to learn to survive in this unusual place.

# Index

# Credits

## Picture Credits

Front Cover – Spine: Clark Wheeler/iStockphoto.com; Top: David Alan Harvey/NGIC; Low Far Left: Nicolas Raynard/NGIC; Low Left: Nicolas Reynard/NGIC; Low Right: Richard Nowitz/NGIC; Low Far Right: Roy Toft/NGIC.

Interior – Alamy: Artesub: 22 lo; Lena Trindade/Brazil Pictures: 23 lo; Corbis: Theo Allofs: 2 right, 10 up, 16-17, 21 lo; Arcaid: 34 lo; Ricardo Azoury: 30 lo, Jamil Bittar: 13 lo; Barnabas Bosshart: 13 up; Owen Franken: 47 center; Paulo Fridman: 3 right, 40 up, 48-49; Larry Dale Gordon/Zefa: 28 up; Ralf Hirschberger/dpa: 41 lo; Stephanie Maze: 35 up, 57 lo; Andre Luis Mello/epa: 44 up; Kadu Niemeyer: 50 lo; Richard Nowitz: 2 left, 6-7, Alessia Paradisi: 46 up; Reuters: 26 up, 35 lo, 57 up; Ricky Rogers/Reuters: 31 up, 56 lo; Galen Rowell: 12 up; George Tiedemann: 45; NGIC: Sam Abell: 54 up, James P. Blair: 29 up, 33 lo; Robert Clark: 53 lo; Dean Conger: 33 up; Nicole Duplaix: 18 lo; MacDuff Everton: 30 up, 32 up; Stuart Franklin: TP, 3 left, 15 lo, 36-37; Bobby Haas: 42 lo, 56 up; David Alan Harvey: 42up, 43 up; Otis Imboden: 20 up; O. Louis Mazzatenta: 53 up; Stephanie Maze: 5 up; Michael Melford: 45 up; George F. Mobley: 15 up; Mark W. Moffett: 38 up; Nicholas Reynard: 11 up, 12 lo, 46 lo; Joel Sartore: 14 lo, 20 lo, 22 up; Frank & Helen Schreider: 28 lo; James L. Stanfield: 2-3, 24-25; Roy Toft: 54 lo; Paul Zahl:21 up; Photos.com: 59 up

For more information, please call 1-800-NGS-LINE (647-5463) or write to the following address:

NATIONAL GEOGRAPHIC SOCIETY
1145 17th Street N.W.
Washington, D.C. 20036-4688 U.S.A.

Visit us at www.nationalgeographic.com

Library of Congress Cataloging-in-Publication Data available on request
ISBN: 978-1-4263-0298-5

Printed in the United States of America

Series design by Jim Hiscott.
The body text is set in Avenir; Knockout.
The display text is set in Matrix Script.

Front Cover—Top: Dancers take part in Carnival in Salvador; Low Far Left: Itaquai River in Amazonia; Low Left: A Matis Indian acts as a guide; Low Right: Sunrise over Rio de Janeiro; Low Far Right: Hyacinth macaws

Page 1—Children's water aerobics class in São Paolo; Icon image on spine, Contents page, and throughout: Plumage

## Produced through the worldwide resources of the National Geographic Society

John M. Fahey, Jr., President and Chief Executive Officer; Gilbert M. Grosvenor, Chairman of the Board; Tim T. Kelly, President of Global Media Group; John Q. Griffin, President, Publishing; Nina D. Hoffman, Executive Vice President, President of Book Publishing Group

### National Geographic Staff for this Book

Nancy Laties Feresten, Vice President, Editor-in-Chief of Children's Books
Bea Jackson, Director of Design and Illustration
Jim Hiscott, Art Director
Virginia Koeth, Project Editor
Lori Epstein, Illustrations Editor
Stacy Gold, Nadia Hughes, Illustrations Research Editors
Grace Hill, Associate Managing Editor
R. Gary Colbert, Production Director
Lewis R. Bassford, Production Manager
Nicole Elliott, Manufacturing Manager
Maps, Mapping Specialists, Ltd.

### Brown Reference Group plc. Staff for this Book

Volume Editor: Tom Jackson
Designer: Dave Allen
Picture Manager: Clare Newman
Maps: Martin Darlison
Artwork: Darren Awuah
Index: Kay Ollerenshaw
Senior Managing Editor: Tim Cooke
Children's Publisher: Anne O'Daly
Editorial Director: Lindsey Lowe

## About the Author

ZILAH DECKKER was born and raised in Brazil. She trained as an architectural historian before moving to the United Kingdom, where she earned a PhD from the University of East Anglia. She has contributed to many publications, including academic encyclopedias on a range of subjects. Her books include Brazil Built: The Architecture of the Modern Movement in Brazil. She lives in London with her young family.

## About the Consultants

DAVID J. ROBINSON is Dellplain Professor of Latin American Geography at Syracuse University, New York. He previously taught at University College London. His research focuses on the historical and developmental geography of Latin America. He is a former Fulbright research fellow to Brazil. He has published six books and edited seven more on a variety of Latin American topics, the most recent of which is Migration in Colonial Hispanic America (Cambridge, 2006).

JOÃO CEZAR DE CASTRO ROCHA is Professor of Transatlantic Comparative Studies at the University of Manchester, where he is course director of the MA in Latin American Cultural Studies. He is the author of four books and has edited 18 books, among which are Brazil 2001: A Revisionary History of Brazilian Literature and Culture and The Author as Plagiarist—The Case of Machado de Assis.

# Time Line of
# Brazilian History

## B.C.

**ca 30,000** Ancient peoples living in Brazil make pottery.

## A.D.

**ca 400** Amerindians make artistic pottery on the island of Marajó at the mouth of the Amazon.

## 1400

**1494** Spain and Portugal sign the Treaty of Tordesillas, an agreement to divide the New World between the two countries. Portugal receives control of the area of Brazil.

## 1500

**1500** Pedro Álvares Cabral, a Portuguese explorer, lands on Brazil's easternmost point and claims the territory for Portugal.

**ca 1530** Sugarcane is introduced to Brazil.

**1532** The Portuguese colonies, São Vicente and Piratininga, are established in southern Brazil.

**1549** Tomé de Sousa becomes governor general of Brazil and governs the fifteen captaincies from Salvador.

**1580** King Philip II of Spain gains the Portuguese crown, which unites Spain and Portugal and brings Brazil under Spanish rule.

## 1600

**1621** The Spanish create the states of Maranhão and Brazil.

**1624** The Dutch take control of São Salvador de Bahia and begin a thirty-year fight to take over northeastern Brazil.

**1640** Portugal declares independence from Spain and Brazil falls under Portuguese rule again.

**1654** The Treaty of Taborda forces the Dutch to return northeastern Brazil to Portuguese control.

**1690** Gold is discovered in Minas Gerais, which leads to a century of mining in the interior of Brazil.

## 1700

**1750** The Treaty of Madrid replaces the Treaty of Tordesillas and establishes geographic boundaries for the territory of Brazil that roughly correspond to the country's current area.

**1763** The capital moves from São Salvador de Bahia to Rio de Janeiro as Brazil's economic focus moves from sugar to gold.

**1792** After a three-year effort to establish a republic, the Inconfidência Mineira movement ends when its leader, Tiradentes, is hanged.

## 1800

**1807** After Napoleon leads a French invasion of Portugal, King João VI flees to Brazil. He rules until 1821 and opens its ports to foreign trade.

**1815** Brazil becomes a united kingdom with Portugal.

**1822** Pedro I, the son of King João VI, declares Brazil independent from